HAWAI'I COOKS *with* PINEAPPLE

Mutual Publishing

All recipes originally appeared in *Hawai'i's Favorite Pineapple Recipes* by Joannie Dobbs and Betty Shimabukuro, © 2002 by Mutual Publishing

ISBN: 978-1-949307-67-2

Design by Jane Gillespie
First Printing, March 2025

Mutual Publishing, LLC
1215 Center Street, Suite 210
Honolulu, Hawai'i 96816
Ph: (808) 732-1709 • Fax: (808) 734-4094
email: info@mutualpublishing.com
www.mutualpublishing.com

Printed in South Korea

CONTENTS

SIMPLY SAVORY 49

ON THE SIDE 71

DESSERTS 81

INTRODUCTION

If the state of Hawai'i were to get a tattoo, it would be in the image of a pineapple. More photographic than a coconut, the pineapple has grown into the universal symbol of these Islands.

Yet the pineapple is non-native. Hawaiians called it hala kahiki—hala after the prickly fruit of the hala tree, also called pandanus or screw pine; kahiki meaning "foreign country."

The fruit hails from South America and likely ended up on the Island of Hawai'i in the sixteenth century, following the shipwreck of a Spanish vessel carrying goods from Mexico. A small, fibrous, and highly acidic variety eventually took root and became known as the Wild Kailua.

In 1882, James Kidwell, an English horticulturist and retired sea captain, began experimenting with several varieties of pineapple in Mānoa, on land that eventually became the University of Hawai'i's flagship campus. Kidwell was never commercially successful, but his contributions earned him the title, "Father of the Pineapple."

Most of the pineapple trade before the turn of the twentieth century involved fresh pineapple, which suffered a high rate of spoilage when shipped. But early canned products were so unstable that cans would occasionally explode. Plus, the United States collected a prohibitively high tariff on canned pineapple.

With annexation, however, came the end of the tariffs, and pineapple got its chance. In 1901, James Dole, a young man with a degree in business and $1,000 to spend, formed Hawaiian Pineapple Co. (now Dole Food Co.). In 1906, he built a cannery in Iwilei. With its 100,000-gallon pineapple-shaped water tank on the roof, the cannery became a landmark and grew into the largest in the world.

The industry spread to Maui, Hawai'i, Kaua'i and, of course, Lāna'i. Dole purchased most of Lāna'i in 1922, turning it into a mega-plantation. By 1950, more than half of the world's pineapple came from Hawai'i.

For years, pineapple and sugar were Hawai'i's leading industries, only to suffer twin fates. The development of farming in countries with lower production costs—Mexico and the Philippines, primarily—cost the state its competitive edge.

Hawai'i now produces less than fifteen percent of the world's supply of pineapple. Lāna'i has been transformed from the Pineapple Island into a luxury resort. The Dole water tower has been dismantled and the cannery turned into a shopping/entertainment complex; Dole's O'ahu North Shore plantation is now a tourist attraction featuring the world's largest maze. The industry perseveres, however. Development of lower-acid varieties continues, with Sugarloaf, Hawaiian Gold, white, and organic pineapples gaining footholds in restaurants and specialty markets. Processed foods bearing local labels—such as pineapple sauces, salsas, and drinks—also guarantee that the prickly pine will continue to be associated with the Islands of Hawai'i.

PINEAPPLE USES

The pineapple is a formidable fruit, armor-plated and prickly. It can seem impenetrable on first approach. There's gold inside, though, so breaking in is worth the struggle.

Pineapples do not sweeten once picked; therefore, they must be harvested ripe. To select one, don't go by color. A ripe fruit may still be mottled green and brown. It should have a deep, sweet scent and give off a solid thunk when flicked. Pick one that is slightly soft, with a compact crown. If the pineapple is kept a few days before eating, its acids will mellow, but the fruit will not get any more ripe or sweet.

To trim, take a very sharp knife and cut off the crown. Then cut a slice off the bottom so it will stand firm. Cut off the skin in thin slices from top to bottom. The fibrous eyes will remain; cut them out in diagonal grooves, spiraling around the fruit. The fruit can then be cut into wedges, round slices, or chunks. Don't cut off the core; it can be the sweetest part. Another method is to quarter the fruit, then slice off the skin, piece-by-piece. Fresh pineapple may also be purchased pre-cut.

Canned pineapple is available packed in unsweetened juice or in syrup. Read recipes carefully to see which is needed; results will vary greatly. Fresh pineapple may be pickled or turned into jam. To can, simmer 10 minutes in water, sugar syrup, apple or fruit juice, then fill jars and process. To freeze, pack fruit tightly into a container with ½-inch space on top. If desired, sweeten with a syrup made from equal parts water and sugar. Crushed fruit and juice (unsweetened or with granulated sugar added) may also be frozen.

SALADS

TROPICAL MIXED FRUIT SALAD

Serves 4

2 tablespoons honey
¼ cup Cream Salad Dressing (see p. 14)
¼ cup Hot Pepper Dressing (see p. 14)
1 cup crushed pineapple
1 cup sliced banana
1 cup diced papaya
1 cup melon pieces (½-inch cubes)
Lettuce leaves
Cayenne pepper or nutmeg, to taste

Combine honey and dressings and let flavors infuse for about 1 hour in the refrigerator.

Toss together fruit and arrange on lettuce; sprinkle with a little cayenne pepper or a little grated nutmeg.

CREAM SALAD DRESSING

Makes about ⅓ cup

¼ cup heavy whipping cream
⅛ teaspoon kosher salt
1 teaspoon granulated sugar
Pinch of black pepper
1 tablespoon white cider vinegar

Beat cream until it thickens. Stir in salt, sugar, and pepper and mix well. Slowly add and beat in the vinegar. Refrigerate.

HOT PEPPER DRESSING

Makes about ⅓ cup

2 tablespoons olive oil
½ teaspoon salt
¼ teaspoon cayenne pepper
⅛ teaspoon granulated sugar
2 tablespoons white cider vinegar

Place ingredients in a small jar, cover tightly, and chill thoroughly in the refrigerator. Shake vigorously for 1 or 2 minutes, just before serving.

PINEAPPLE CABBAGE SALAD

Serves 4

3 cups shredded cabbage
1 cup grated carrots
1 cup crushed pineapple
⅛ cup packed raisins
2 tablespoons mayonnaise
¼ tablespoon Japanese rice vinegar
½ teaspoon fresh lime juice
⅛ teaspoon finely minced Hawaiian chili pepper
Salt and pepper, to taste

GARNISH
Chopped peanuts

In a large bowl, combine cabbage, carrots, pineapple, and raisins. Set aside.

In a cup, combine mayonnaise, rice vinegar, lime juice, and chili pepper.

Toss with salad and serve with a garnish of chopped peanuts.

WARM PINEAPPLE SPINACH SALAD

Serves 4

Pineapple Dressing
1 pound spinach leaves
2 cups button mushrooms
1 cup diced pineapple

GARNISH
Chopped macadamia nuts or minced cooked bacon

Prepare Pineapple Dressing and set aside to simmer until just before serving. Clean all vegetables and slice mushrooms.

In a large serving bowl, toss vegetables and diced pineapple with the freshly made warm dressing. Place on salad plates and sprinkle with macadamia nuts or bacon.

PINEAPPLE DRESSING

Makes about 1 cup

¾ cup pineapple juice
2 tablespoons champagne vinegar
¼ cup diced pineapple
½ teaspoon kosher salt

Combine all ingredients in a blender and pulse-blend until smooth. Just before serving, pour into a saucepan and heat until it simmers.

PINEAPPLE CHICKEN SALAD

Serves 2

2 (6-ounce) skinless, boneless chicken breasts
2 teaspoons olive oil
2 tablespoons minced onion
1 cup pineapple cubes
½ cup diced celery
4 large pitted black olives, minced
¼ cup regular or low-fat ranch dressing
8 leaves butterhead or any bibb lettuce, rinsed and dried

GARNISH

2 tablespoons chopped macadamia nuts

Rinse and dry chicken breasts. Slice into bite-size strips of about ½-inch thick and place in a small bowl. Toss with olive oil. Heat small skillet to hot and sear chicken about 30 to 45 seconds on each side (until the pink is just gone). Remove to a plate. Add onion to the skillet and heat until translucent.

In a large bowl, toss pineapple, chicken, celery, onion, and minced olives together. Dab ranch dressing over top of salad and toss again. Spoon pineapple chicken salad onto lettuce cups and garnish with macadamia nuts.

CURRIED PINEAPPLE TURKEY SALAD

Serves 4

2 cups cold cooked rice
1 cup diced cooked turkey
½ cup sliced celery
¼ cup diced green bell pepper
½ cup canned pineapple chunks, drained
½ cup mayonnaise
2 teaspoons curry powder
⅛ teaspoon kosher salt
⅛ teaspoon ground ginger
8 red leaf lettuce leaves

GARNISH

Chopped and seeded Roma tomato

In a large bowl, combine rice, turkey, celery, bell pepper, and pineapple chunks. Toss; set aside. In a small bowl, whisk together mayonnaise, curry powder, salt, and ginger. Add to turkey mixture and mix thoroughly. Cover and refrigerate 2 to 3 hours, or overnight.

Just before serving, wash lettuce and place on salad plates. Spoon turkey mixture onto salad greens and garnish with chopped tomatoes.

PINEAPPLE CRAB SALAD

Serves 4

2 cups chunky crab meat
½ cup mayonnaise
1 teaspoon Worcestershire sauce
2 to 3 teaspoons Old Bay Spice
1 tablespoon ketchup
2 cups diced fresh pineapple or canned (well-drained)
12 Mānoa lettuce leaves or other bibb lettuce
2 Roma tomatoes, seeded and diced
Kosher salt and pepper, to taste, or approximately ⅛ teaspoon each

In a medium bowl, combine crab, mayonnaise, Worcestershire, Old Bay Spice, and ketchup. Once thoroughly mixed, add pineapple and toss.

Place three lettuce leaves per plate and top with a mound of crab mixture. Sprinkle with diced tomatoes and salt and black pepper, to taste.

PINEAPPLE SLAW WITH FETA CHEESE

Serves 4

- 1 cup minced fresh or canned pineapple
- 2 cups shredded carrot
- 1 green pepper, julienned
- 3 tablespoons white wine vinegar
- 3 tablespoons pineapple juice
- 1 tablespoon honey
- 1 teaspoon canola oil
- 8 tablespoons crumbled feta cheese or 4 tablespoons each feta and blue cheese

In a large bowl, toss together pineapple, carrot, and green pepper. Set aside.

In a small bowl, whisk together vinegar, pineapple juice, honey, and canola oil. Pour over slaw mixture and toss. Cover and chill 1 hour. Top with feta and blue cheese just before serving.

SALSAS

SIMPLE PINEAPPLE MANGO SALSA

Makes about 2 cups

1 (14-ounce) can pineapple chunks in juice, drained

1 cup mango chutney (or any fruit chutney)

1 to 2 teaspoons jerk seasoning (see note)

Combine drained pineapple with chutney. Add jerk seasoning a little at a time and pulse in a food processor until the desired consistency is reached. Do Not Purée.

Serve with tortilla or taro chips or chilled sliced cucumbers.

Note: Jerk seasonings vary greatly, add carefully.

TOTALLY TROPICAL FRUIT SALSA

Makes about 2 cups

¼ cup minced fresh pineapple
¼ cup minced papaya
¼ cup minced mango
¼ cup minced kiwi
¼ cup minced red bell pepper
⅓ cup minced red onion
2 tablespoons minced red chili pepper
¼ cup minced cilantro or mint (see note)
2 tablespoons fresh lime juice
½ teaspoon kosher salt
⅛ teaspoon coarse black pepper

Clean fruit and vegetables, mince, and toss together in a medium mixing bowl. Season with lime juice and salt and pepper. Refrigerate until chilled.

Note: Cilantro and mint can be used together with the total equaling ¼ cup minced herb.

ROASTED PINEAPPLE MANGO SALSA

Makes about 3 cups

- 1 cup diced roasted pineapple
- 1 cup diced mango
- ¼ cup diced red onion
- ½ small red bell pepper, sliced into ½-inch lengths
- ½ small green bell pepper, sliced into ½-inch lengths
- 1 red chili pepper without seeds, minced
- 2 tablespoons lime juice
- ⅛ teaspoon salt
- 1 teaspoon granulated sugar

To roast the pineapple, preheat oven to 350°F. Remove pineapple skin and slice lengthwise—approximately ¼-inch thick. Spread out on a sheet pan and bake for approximately 20 to 25 minutes, or until the pineapple releases its liquid. Remove pineapple center core and dice. Refrigerate until cool.

In a mixing bowl, combine roasted pineapple, mango, onion, bell peppers, chili pepper, and lime juice; mix together. Season with salt and sug-

ar and mix again. Cover and refrigerate overnight and use within three days.

PINEAPPLE GRAPEFRUIT SALSA

Makes about 4 cups

1 small grapefruit
1 sweet orange
1 cup crushed pineapple in heavy syrup
½ cup diced red onion
1 small red bell pepper, seeded and diced
1 jalapeño pepper, seeded and diced
2 tablespoons sliced green onion tops
¼ teaspoon kosher salt
1 teaspoon olive oil

Peel and segment grapefruit and orange and dice. Place in a medium bowl along with the pineapple, red onion, diced peppers, and green onion tops. Toss. Sprinkle with kosher salt and olive oil and toss again.

CONFETTI PINEAPPLE SALSA

Makes about 3 cups

2 cups diced fresh pineapple or well-drained, canned pineapple chunks
¼ cup diced red onion
¼ cup each diced green and yellow bell pepper
2 tablespoons chopped raisins
1 teaspoon minced garlic clove
1 jalapeño pepper, seeded and minced
½ teaspoon ground coriander
¼ teaspoon ground cumin
⅛ teaspoon kosher salt

GARNISH

2 Roma tomatoes, seeded and diced

In a medium bowl, combine and fold together pineapple, onion, bell pepper, garlic, and raisins.

In a cup, combine jalapeño, coriander, cumin, and salt and sprinkle over pineapple mixture. Toss until spices are evenly distributed. Cover and refrigerate overnight. Garnish with freshly diced tomatoes.

PINEAPPLE GINGER SALSA

Makes about 2 cups

1½ cups chopped pineapple
½ cup diced red onion
1 minced jalapeño chili, seeded
1 tablespoon finely grated fresh ginger
Zest of 1 lime
1 tablespoon fresh lime juice
½ cup chopped cilantro or American parsley, divided use
Salt and pepper, to taste

In a small bowl, combine pineapple, onion and jalapeño. Toss and add ginger, lime zest, lime juice, and 3 tablespoons chopped cilantro. Toss again. Transfer to serving bowl and sprinkle with remaining 1 tablespoon cilantro. Cover and refrigerate for a few hours to allow flavors to infuse.

SWEET, SOUR & SAVORY

VIETNAMESE SWEET AND SOUR SAUCE

Makes about 1 cup

2 shallots, minced
2 cloves garlic, minced
2 teaspoons canola oil
½ teaspoon ground chili paste
1 tablespoon ketchup
2 teaspoons fish sauce
2 teaspoons granulated sugar
½ cup chopped tomatoes
¼ cup chicken stock or canned low-sodium chicken broth
1 tablespoon cornstarch
3 tablespoons water
¼ teaspoon fresh lemon juice

In a saucepan over moderate heat, sauté shallots and garlic in oil until just golden. Mix in chili paste, ketchup, fish sauce, and sugar and stir for 1 minute. Add the tomatoes and chicken stock and cook over low heat until slightly reduced, about 3 to 5 minutes.

Stir water into cornstarch and add 1 teaspoon at a time to sauce, stir until sauce is just slightly thickened. Stir lemon juice into the sauce and remove from heat.

COLD SWEET AND SOUR SOUP

Makes about 6 cups

1 tablespoon olive oil
1 cup chopped Maui or red onion
2 cups chopped cabbage
6 ounces V8 juice
2 cups water
⅓ cup fresh lemon juice
¼ cup honey
Salt and pepper, to taste
⅓ cup pineapple juice

Heat oil and sauté onions over low heat until translucent and caramelized. Add cabbage and sauté for about 5 additional minutes until completely limp. Stir in V8, water, lemon juice, and honey and simmer for 15 to 20 minutes. Season with salt and pepper and remove from heat.

Cool soup and then pour into a blender or food processor and purée to a smooth consistency. Refrigerate overnight. Just before serving, mix in pineapple juice.

SWEET AND SOUR TOFU STIR-FRY

Makes 4 servings

½ cup pineapple juice
1 tablespoon dark brown sugar
¼ cup apple juice concentrate
1 tablespoon rice vinegar
2 tablespoons peanut oil (or canola oil)
1 tablespoon finely chopped and peeled ginger root
2 tablespoons peeled and minced garlic
1 Hawaiian chili pepper, seeded and minced
4 cups frozen Asian stir-fry vegetables (see note)
20 ounces firm or extra firm regular tofu, drained, cut into ½-inch slices
2 Roma tomatoes, diced
1 cup canned straw mushrooms, drained
1 tablespoon cornstarch mixed with 2 tablespoons water to thicken
Salt and freshly ground pepper, to taste

In a small bowl, combine pineapple juice, brown sugar, apple juice and rice vinegar. Set aside.

Heat peanut or canola oil in a wok or heavy skillet and add ginger, garlic, and chili pepper. Stir-fry for about 1 minute. Add frozen vegetables and stir-fry for 3 minutes more. Add the tofu, tomato, and mushrooms and add cornstarch mixture, if necessary, to thicken. Season to taste with salt and pepper. Turn onto a platter and serve.

Note: Asian vegetable mixes are always colorful and contain many flavors and textures. Mixes include varying combinations of bamboo shoots, bell peppers, broccoli, carrots, baby corn cobs, leeks, mushrooms, onions, and water chestnuts.

SOOO SIMPLE SWEET AND SOUR CHICKEN

Serves 6

Pineapple Marinade
(see p. 39)
2 pounds boneless, skinless chicken tenderloin fillets

GARNISH
Chopped Roma tomatoes

Place chicken fillets in a glass baking dish. Pour sauce over chicken, making sure that all pieces are coated. Cover casserole and marinate chicken in the refrigerator overnight.

Preheat oven to 325°F. Bake for 1 hour. Serve with a sprinkle of freshly chopped tomatoes on top.

PINEAPPLE MARINADE

Makes about 1½ cups

1 (1-ounce) package French onion soup mix
½ cup pineapple preserves (or apricot pineapple preserves)
1 cup French, Russian, or Catalina salad dressing

In a small bowl, stir together soup mix, pineapple preserves, and salad dressing. Refrigerate until used.

BASIC SWEET AND SOUR PINEAPPLE SAUCE

Makes about 1½ cups

⅔ cup heavy syrup from canned pineapple
⅓ cup cider vinegar
2 tablespoons water
¼ cup soy sauce
1 tablespoon ketchup
2 tablespoons cornstarch
2 tablespoons granulated sugar

In a saucepan, combine all sauce ingredients. Bring mixture to a boil, stirring until thick. Use as a dip or pour over your entrée or vegetable.

SWEET AND SOUR CHICKEN KEBABS

Serves 4

- Basic Sweet and Sour Pineapple Sauce (see p. 39)
- 1 (20-ounce) can pineapple chunks
- 4 skinless, boneless chicken thighs
- 2 medium green bell peppers, cored, seeded, and cut into 2-inch squares
- 1 onion, cut in 1-inch chunks
- 8 skewers

Preheat oven to 425°F. Spray a baking pan with vegetable oil spray. Over a small bowl, drain pineapple and reserve juice. Rinse chicken and pat dry; cut into 1-inch stew-cut cubes. Place chicken in reserved pineapple juice.

To create kebabs, alternate chicken, green pepper, onion and pineapple on skewers; then brush each kebab with Sweet and Sour Sauce. Place in a baking pan and bake for 10 to 12 minutes, or until sizzling.

SWEET AND SOUR MEATBALLS

Serves 4

SWEET AND SOUR MEATBALL SAUCE
1 (20-ounce) can pineapple chunks in heavy syrup
⅔ cup water, divided use
3 tablespoons distilled white vinegar
1 tablespoon soy sauce
½ cup packed brown sugar
3 tablespoons cornstarch
½ teaspoon ground ginger
½ teaspoon salt

1 pound lean ground beef
1 large egg
½ cup dry bread crumbs
¼ cup finely chopped onion
1 teaspoon granulated sugar
¼ teaspoon ground ginger
¼ teaspoon salt
¼ teaspoon ground black pepper
1 teaspoon Worcestershire sauce
1 large carrot, diagonally sliced
1 large green bell pepper, seeded and cut into ½-inch pieces

To make the Sweet and Sour Meatball Sauce, drain pineapple and reserve syrup. Set aside pineapple chunks to add later. Mix pineapple syrup with enough water to make 1 cup; add to a large sauce pan. Stir in vinegar, soy sauce, and brown sugar and bring to a simmer.

In a separate cup, mix together cornstarch, ginger and salt. Mix water into cornstarch mixture and add to sauce. Stir until smooth. Cover and cook over medium heat until thickened.

To make the meatballs, preheat oven to 400°F and lightly spray a large baking sheet with vegetable oil.

In a large bowl, thoroughly mix beef, egg, bread crumbs and onion. Create a well in the meat mixture center and combine sugar, ginger, salt, pepper, and Worcestershire sauce; thoroughly mix into meatball mixture. Shape into 1-inch balls and place a single layer on a baking sheet. Bake for 10 to 15 minutes.

Add pineapple chunks, carrot, green pepper, and meatballs into the sauce; gently stir to evenly coat. Simmer uncovered until meatballs are thoroughly cooked (about 20 minutes).

SWEET AND SOUR PORK

Serves 4

1 pound pork tenderloin
1 tablespoon cornstarch
2 teaspoons canola oil, divided use
1 small thumb fresh ginger, thinly sliced
1 cup chopped green bell pepper
1 (20-ounce) can pineapple chunks in heavy syrup
2 tablespoons white vinegar
1 tablespoon soy sauce
2 tablespoons tomato paste

Cut tenderloin into bite-size pieces and toss with cornstarch.

In a wok or heavy skillet, heat 1 teaspoon canola oil to high and fry meat until golden brown. Remove meat and set aside.

Add remaining oil, ginger slices and bell pepper to wok. Drain pineapple and reserve syrup. Add pineapple syrup, vinegar, soy sauce, and tomato paste to wok; stir. Heat to a simmer. Add back pork and pineapple chunks and stir well; simmer until sauce is reduced.

SWEET AND SOUR SHRIMP

Serves 4

1 cup teriyaki sauce
⅓ cup pineapple juice
1 tablespoon rice vinegar
¼ teaspoon hot sauce
¼ teaspoon cornstarch
2 teaspoons canola oil
1 teaspoon peeled and minced fresh ginger
1 cup fresh pineapple chunks
2 tablespoons minced green onion
2 cups (1½-inch pieces) long beans or fresh young green beans
1 pound fresh or frozen peeled and deveined shrimp

GARNISH

Sprinkle of toasted sesame seed

Whisk together teriyaki sauce, pineapple juice, vinegar, and hot sauce. Mix into cornstarch and set aside.

In a saucepan, heat oil and sauté ginger. Add pineapple chunks and green onion and heat until pineapple begins to brown. Stir occasionally. Add teriyaki-pineapple mixture and long beans. Simmer for about 5 minutes.

In a separate heavy skillet or wok, heat oil and sauté shrimp until they just turn pink. Add to sauce and remove from heat.

Serve over a bed of rice and garnish with toasted sesame seeds.

SWEET AND SOUR 'AHI TUNA

Serves 4

4 (6-ounce) 'ahi (yellowfin) tuna fillets
1 tablespoon canola oil
Salt and freshly ground pepper, to taste
1 cup diced red bell pepper
1 cup diced green bell pepper
1 cup rinsed and sliced shiitake mushrooms
1 cup sliced button mushrooms
1 cup mung bean sprouts
2 cups diced fresh pineapple
1 cup stew-cut papaya
Sweet and Sour Citrus Sauce (see p. 48)

GARNISH

½ cup green onion tops and a sprinkle of black sesame seeds

Rinse fish fillet and pat dry with paper towels.

Heat a large, dry cast-iron skillet over high heat. Brush fillets lightly with canola oil and season fish with salt and pepper. Cook about 3 minutes. Using a large spatula, turn and cook other side until desired doneness, about 3 to 4 minutes for rare. Remove to a plate.

Add bell peppers, mushrooms, and bean sprouts to the skillet and stir-fry for about 15 seconds. Add pineapple and papaya and stir-fry for an additional 30 seconds. Pour Sweet and Sour Citrus Sauce into the skillet and toss until all vegetables are evenly coated.

Plate fish and ladle sweet and sour vegetable mixture over fillet. Garnish with green onion and black sesame seeds.

SWEET AND SOUR CITRUS SAUCE

Makes about 1 cup

1 cup orange juice
¼ cup cider vinegar
1 (1-inch) piece fresh ginger, peeled and minced
½ cup ketchup
1 tablespoon cornstarch, dissolved in ¼ cup cold water

In a medium saucepan, combine the orange juice, vinegar, and ginger. Simmer for 5 minutes and add ketchup and cornstarch mixture. Stir over medium heat until sauce is thickened, about 3 minutes. Set aside.

SIMPLY SAVORY

SESAME CHICKEN IN PINEAPPLE SAUCE

Serves 4

- 4 skinless, boneless chicken breasts
- 1 teaspoon toasted sesame oil
- 1 teaspoon peanut oil
- 2 cups crushed pineapple
- 2 cups chicken stock or canned low-sodium chicken broth
- 1 tablespoon brandy
- 1 teaspoon soy sauce
- 1 tablespoon cornstarch
- 2 tablespoons water

GARNISH

Toasted sesame seeds

Rinse chicken and pat dry. Heat sesame and peanut oils in a heavy skillet or wok and sear chicken on both sides until brown. Add pineapple, chicken stock, brandy, and soy sauce and heat to simmering.

Mix together cornstarch and water and combine with chicken to create the sauce. Heat for 3 more minutes, stirring constantly. Transfer to a serving bowl and sprinkle with toasted sesame seeds.

CURRIED PINEAPPLE-MANGO CHICKEN

Serves 4

3 skinless, boneless chicken breasts
4 teaspoons sunflower oil, divided use
1 cup sliced onion
2 tablespoons peeled and minced ginger
2 tablespoons curry powder
1 teaspoon cinnamon
⅓ cup raisins
3 tablespoons mango chutney
½ cup orange juice
2 cups fresh pineapple chunks
Salt and pepper, to taste

Slice chicken into ½-inch thick strips and place in a small bowl. Toss with 2 teaspoons sunflower oil; set aside. Heat skillet to hot and sear chicken for about 30 to 45 seconds on each side (until pink is just gone). Remove to a plate. Add remaining oil and sauté onions and ginger together over medium heat until onions are translucent and caramelized. Remove to a plate. Add curry powder, cinnamon, raisins, mango chutney, orange juice, and pineapple and heat until it just reaches a boil. Return chicken to sauce, stir and cover for about 2 minutes. Serve over rice.

CRUNCHY PINEAPPLE CHICKEN

Serves 4

4 skinless, boneless chicken breasts or thighs
1 tablespoon peanut oil
1 medium onion, rough chopped
4 stalks celery, rough chopped
1 (5-ounce) can water chestnuts, drained
1 red bell pepper, sliced into strips
2 tablespoons water
1 tablespoon soy sauce
1 tablespoon cornstarch
1 cup crushed pineapple in syrup
¼ cup chopped peanuts
Salt, to taste

Rinse and pat dry chicken breasts and slice into ½-inch thick strips. Set aside.

In a skillet or wok, heat oil and add chicken. Sauté chicken until just pink and transfer chicken to a plate. Add onion, celery, water chestnuts, and bell pepper to the skillet and sauté until onion becomes translucent.

Meanwhile, mix water and soy sauce into cornstarch to make a slurry. Add to vegetable mixture, along with pineapple, syrup, and peanuts and stir for 2 minutes, or until sauce becomes thick. Add chicken and cook for 1 more minute only.

Serve immediately over white or brown rice.

HOT AND SPICY PINEAPPLE PORK

Serves 4

- 1 pound pork loin
- 2 tablespoons soy sauce
- 1½ tablespoons peeled and minced fresh ginger
- 1 teaspoon peeled and minced garlic
- 2 teaspoons canola oil
- 2 tablespoons chicken broth or canned low-sodium chicken broth
- 1¼ cups cider vinegar
- 3 tablespoons packed brown sugar
- 2 tablespoons cornstarch
- 1 teaspoon minced hot chili pepper
- 2 celery stalks, crescent-sliced
- 1¼ cups diced pineapple in heavy syrup
- ¼ cup pineapple juice
- ¼ cup diced cashews or walnuts

Slice pork and place in a flat-bottomed casserole. Combine soy sauce, ginger and garlic and pour over pork slices. Cover and marinate pork, refrigerated, for an hour.

In a wok or skillet, heat canola oil to hot and stir-fry pork until browned. Transfer pork to a plate.

Combine broth, vinegar, brown sugar, and cornstarch and chili pepper. Add to wok and stir constantly while simmering. When sauce begins to thicken, add celery, pineapple, and pineapple juice. Once sauce begins to boil, reduce heat and simmer for about 5 minutes. Add pork and chopped nuts and heat a few more minutes.

Serve over rice or couscous.

PINEAPPLE-HONEY MUSTARD-GLAZED PORK CHOPS

Serves 4

3 tablespoons pineapple preserves
3 tablespoons honey mustard
3 tablespoons water
1 teaspoon Worcestershire sauce
4 (4-ounce) boneless pork loin chops (¾-inch thick)
⅛ teaspoon kosher salt
⅛ teaspoon black pepper

GARNISH
Chopped macadamia nuts and fresh chopped parsley

In a small bowl, mix together pineapple preserves, honey mustard, water, and Worcestershire sauce; set aside.

Season chops with salt and pepper and brown chops on both sides over medium-high heat. Add pineapple mixture to the skillet and reduce heat to low. Cover and simmer for about 5 minutes. Garnish with macadamia nuts and parsley. Serve.

SLOW-COOKING PEPPER PINEAPPLE TURKEY STEW

Serves 4

2 cups cooked turkey (see note)
2 large carrots
2 stalks celery
1 large onion
2 large green bell peppers
1 teaspoon canola oil
2 cups water
1 cup pineapple chunks in juice
1 tablespoon packed brown sugar
2 tablespoons soy sauce

GARNISH

Fresh chopped Roma tomatoes

Slice turkey into stew-size pieces. Set aside. Clean carrots, celery, and onion and cut into stew-size pieces. Meanwhile, remove ribs and seeds from bell peppers and cut into 1½ inch strips.

In a large heavy-bottomed pot, add oil, turkey, and vegetables and sauté until brown. Add water to the pot and bring to a simmer until vegetables are nearly cooked. Stir in pineapple chunks, brown sugar, and soy sauce and heat until it reaches a simmer.

Serve over rice with the sprinkle of fresh chopped tomato.

Note: To use uncooked turkey, rinse and cut into 1-inch cubes. In a large heavy-bottomed pot, heat 2 teaspoons of canola oil and brown turkey. Turn heat off and cover.

TROPICAL BEEF KEBABS

Serves 4

- 1 pound boneless top sirloin beef
- ¼ cup canned pineapple juice
- 2 tablespoons distilled white vinegar
- 1 tablespoon molasses
- 1 teaspoon salt
- ⅛ teaspoon ground black pepper
- 1 large Maui onion, cut into 1-inch slices
- 12 fresh or canned pineapple chunks
- 8 firm, ripe cherry tomatoes
- 2 medium-size green bell peppers, seeded, ribbed, and cut into 1-inch strips

Cut beef into 1-inch cubes; set aside. In a large bowl, stir together pineapple juice, vinegar, molasses, salt, and pepper until well-combined. Add beef cubes, cover, and refrigerate for at least 4 hours, turning the beef over occasionally.

Reserving the marinade, remove beef cubes and thread onto skewers. Thread vegetables and fruit onto separate skewers. Dip meat skewers into marinade and grill for 10 minutes. When meat is nearly cooked, grill pineapple and vegetable skewers over hot coals for 5 minutes.

GRILLED PINEAPPLE-GLAZED BEEF SHORT RIBS

Serves 4

- 2 pounds well-trimmed beef short ribs, about ½-inch thick
- ½ teaspoon kosher salt
- ¼ teaspoon ground black pepper
- ¼ cup water
- 1 cup pineapple preserves
- 2 tablespoons packed brown sugar
- ¾ cup chili sauce
- ¼ cup cider vinegar
- ⅓ cup pineapple juice

Season ribs with salt and pepper and place in a Dutch oven with water. Cover and simmer until meat is tender (about 2 hours). If necessary during cooking, add more water. Drain.

Mix together pineapple preserves, brown sugar, chili sauce, vinegar, and pineapple juice.

Prepare grill or preheat broiler.

Brush beef ribs with pineapple glaze, covering them thoroughly. Grill or broil ribs for 10 minutes. Baste ribs with remaining marinade while cooking and cook an additional 4 to 5 minutes. Heat remaining sauce and serve with ribs (see note).

Note: Ribs may be cooked in a covered pan in a 350°F oven for 1½ hours.

PINEAPPLE RAISIN POT ROAST

Serves 6

1 (3 lbs.) blade-cut chuck roast
2 teaspoons kosher salt
2 teaspoons ground cumin
2 teaspoons canola oil
2 cups chopped white onion
6 peeled and minced garlic cloves
½ cup tomato sauce
⅓ cup balsamic vinegar
1 (15-ounce) can sliced black olives
1 cup raisins
1 cup crushed pineapple in heavy syrup

Preheat oven to 190 to 200°F. Dry-rub both sides of meat with salt and cumin. Set aside. Heat a heavy skillet on high heat until very hot. Brown meat on both sides and remove from pan. Lower heat and add canola oil to skillet. Heat onions until translucent and add garlic. Stir for about 30 seconds. Add tomato sauce, vinegar, olives, raisins, and crushed pineapple with syrup. Bring to a boil and simmer until the liquid is reduced by half.

In an oven casserole with lid, place roast and other ingredients and cook until the meat is tender (about 3 hours). Remove from oven and hold meat for at least ½ hour before serving.

HONEY LAMB KEBABS

Serves 4

3-pound leg of lamb
4 thin slices ginger
4 garlic cloves, crushed
3 tablespoons soy sauce
1 cup finely sliced onion
Juice from ½ lemon
3 tablespoons honey
Sprinkle of kosher salt
Sprinkle of freshly ground pepper
1 medium green bell pepper, ribs and seeds removed, cut into 1½-inch strips
3 cups fresh pineapple chunks

Remove lamb meat from bone and slice lengthwise into 1-inch strips and then 1-inch cubes. Combine ginger, garlic, soy sauce, onion, lemon juice and honey. Season with salt and pepper. Place meat in marinade, cover, and refrigerate overnight. Boil remaining used marinade before brushing on cooked lamb.

Preheat broiler. Thread lamb on skewers and lay on tray; broil for about 5 minutes on each side. Thread alternating pieces of pineapple chunks and bell pepper on skewers. Place on a tray and broil for about 2 minutes on each side. For a real flair, slip kebabs off skewers and toss together in a hollowed pineapple shell.

SIMPLY SALMON AND PINEAPPLE PAPAYA SALSA

Serves 4

4 (6-ounce) salmon fillets (about ¾-inch thick)
Light sprinkle of kosher salt and freshly ground black pepper
Pineapple Papaya Salsa

Preheat broiler. Place salmon on a metal baking sheet and sprinkle with salt and pepper. Broil fish until it just starts to firm and is no longer translucent (about 5 minutes). Turn fillets and broil about 1 more minute. Transfer to plates and top with Pineapple Papaya Salsa.

PINEAPPLE PAPAYA SALSA

Makes 2 cups

½ cup diced fresh pineapple
¼ cup minced green bell pepper
½ cup diced papaya

¼ cup diced red or mild white onion
½ cup firm ripe tomato
2 tablespoons fresh lemon juice
½ teaspoon kosher salt
⅛ teaspoon coarse black pepper
1 teaspoon red pepper flakes
1 teaspoon chopped parsley

Clean fruit and vegetables. Dice and gently toss together in a medium mixing bowl. Season with lemon juice, red pepper flakes, salt and pepper. Mix in parsley. Cover and refrigerate until chilled to allow flavors to blend.

CASHEW TOFU

Serves 4

1 (20-ounce) block firm tofu
1 bunch green onion (about 8 stalks)
1 tablespoon canola oil
2 peeled and minced garlic cloves
2 tablespoons oyster sauce
1 (5-ounce) can sliced water chestnuts, drained
½ cup crushed pineapple in heavy syrup
1 teaspoon red chili pepper flakes
½ cup chopped unsalted roasted cashew nuts, divided use

GARNISH
Chopped cashew nuts

Freeze tofu overnight. While still slightly frozen, slice into 1-inch cubes. Set aside. Trim green onion tops to 2-inch lengths. Set aside.

In a wok, heat canola oil and stir-fry garlic briefly until light brown. Add tofu and oyster sauce; then stir-fry for 3 minutes. Stir in water chestnuts, green onion, crushed pineapple, red chili pepper flakes and ⅓ cup roasted cashew nuts. Lightly toss until green onion tops are limp. Chop remaining cashew nuts and sprinkle over tofu dish.

ON THE SIDE

PINEAPPLE-CRANBERRY RELISH

Makes about 5 cups

1 pound cranberries
2 apples
1½ cups granulated sugar
Juice of 1 lemon
1 (20-ounce) can crushed pineapple
2 ounces brandy or Grand Marnier (see note)

Chop cranberries and core apples with skin or briefly pulse-chop cranberries in food processor and manually chop apples. Pour into a glass mixing bowl. Immediately toss with lemon juice to prevent apples from browning. Then add sugar, crushed pineapple and brandy and stir well.

Cover and refrigerate for at least several hours, or overnight. This relish may be frozen for spur-of-the-moment bursts of flavor anytime of the year.

Note: Frozen orange juice concentrate can be substituted for alcohol.

WHIPPED PINEAPPLE YAMS

Makes 4 cups

2 pounds yams, cut into 1-inch slices
1 teaspoon salt
Water for boiling
½ cup packed brown sugar
1 cup buttermilk
½ cup coconut milk
1 (20-ounce) can crushed pineapple in syrup

In a medium saucepan, place yams, enough water to cover, and salt. Bring water to a boil over high heat and reduce heat to a simmer until yams are soft and can be easily pierced with a fork. Drain, cool, and peel.

In a blender or food processor, purée together yams, buttermilk, coconut milk, brown sugar, and crushed pineapple.

Place in a glass casserole and bake at 350°F to rewarm or microwave for about 10 minutes.

PINEAPPLE PECAN STUFFING

Makes 4 cups

2 tablespoons butter
½ cup chopped onion
1 cup minced celery
1 cup chopped pecans
¼ cup finely chopped fresh parsley
1 teaspoon kosher salt
¼ teaspoon white pepper
4 cups bread crumbs
1½ cups vegetable or chicken stock
1 cup crushed pineapple in heavy syrup

Heat butter in a frying pan and sauté onion, celery, and pecans over moderate heat until onion becomes translucent. Stir in parsley, salt, and pepper. Add bread crumbs and mix well.

Pour stock into a large glass bowl and microwave for 2 minutes. Pour into stuffing mixture and stir well to moisten. Spoon stuffing into a 3-quart casserole with lid. Cover and microwave until heated through (about 10 minutes). Let stand, covered for 5 additional minutes.

APRICOT-PINEAPPLE COUSCOUS

Makes 4 cups

1 cup dry couscous
¼ cup diced dried apricots
¼ cup diced dried pineapple
½ teaspoon salt
1½ cups boiling water

GARNISH
Freshly chopped mint

In a large lidded casserole, stir together couscous, apricots, pineapple, and salt. Pour boiling water over couscous and cover. Let rest until liquid is absorbed (about 5 minutes).

Fluff couscous with a fork and serve immediately.

CROCK-POT PINEAPPLE CORNBREAD STUFFING

Makes 4 cups

1 (20-ounce) can crushed pineapple in syrup
¼ cup evaporated milk
2 cups cornbread crumbs
½ cup granulated sugar
¼ cup melted butter
3 eggs, beaten
Vegetable oil spray

In a medium-size mixing bowl, combine crushed pineapple, evaporated milk, and sugar; stir until sugar is dissolved. Mix in cornbread, melted butter, and eggs.

Lightly spray the bottom and sides of a crockpot with vegetable oil spray. Pour in stuffing ingredients, cover, and cook on high for about 2½ hours.

COCONUT THAI RICE

Makes about 4 cups

- 1 cup jasmine or other long-grain rice
- 2 teaspoons canola oil
- 1 cup chopped onion
- 3 peeled and minced garlic cloves
- 1 teaspoon peeled and minced ginger
- 1 (15-ounce) can coconut milk
- 1 cup crushed pineapple with liquid
- ¾ cup water
- ½ teaspoon kosher salt

Rinse jasmine or long-grain rice under cold running water until water runs clear. Let drain. Set aside.

In a large saucepan, heat oil over medium heat and sauté onion and ginger until onion is translucent. Add garlic and stir for about 30 seconds. Stir in rice and pineapple and cover. Reduce heat to low and simmer until rice is tender and liquid is absorbed (about 20 minutes). Remove from heat and stir in coconut milk. Let stand, covered, for 5 minutes. Sprinkle salt over rice and distribute by tossing with a fork.

PINEAPPLE FRIED RICE

Makes about 6 cups

2 tablespoons peanut oil
4 ounces Chinese sausages, cut diagonally into ¼-inch slices
½ cup diced onion
1 tablespoon peeled and minced garlic
2 eggs, lightly beaten
4 cups cold cooked long-grain rice
2 tablespoons soy sauce
1 tablespoon fish sauce
1 cup diced pineapple

GARNISH

1 bunch green onion, sliced into 2-inch pieces

In a large, heavy skillet or wok, heat peanut oil, Chinese sausages, and onion over medium-high heat; stir-fry until onion is translucent. Stir in garlic for about 10 seconds and then stir in eggs for about 1 minute. Decrease heat to medium. Stir in rice and sauté for 2 minutes. Mix together soy sauce, fish sauce, and pineapple and add to rice. Sauté until heated through.

In a separate small skillet, lightly sauté green onion until limp; mix half with fried rice and sprinkle the rest on top.

TROPICAL MIXED BEANS

Makes 4 cups

1 (15-ounce) can garbanzo beans
1 (15-ounce) can kidney beans
1 red onion, chopped
2 teaspoons canola oil
4 cloves garlic, minced
1 (20-ounce) can pineapple chunks
2 tablespoons packed brown sugar
1 tablespoon fresh lime juice
½ teaspoon kosher salt
½ teaspoon black pepper
2 cups seeded and chopped fresh tomatoes

Drain beans, rinse, and drain again. Set aside. In a large saucepan, sauté onion in canola oil until onions are translucent. Add garlic and stir for 1 minute. Drain pineapple and add to onion, along with beans, brown sugar, lime juice, salt, and pepper. Stir and simmer for approximately 15 minutes. Add more water if mixture becomes too thick. Cool and then cover and refrigerate over night.

Just before serving, stir in 1½ cups chopped tomatoes. Sprinkle the remaining tomato on top as a garnish.

DESSERTS

PINEAPPLE UPSIDE-DOWN CAKE

Serves 12 to 16

¾ cup brown sugar
½ cup butter, divided use
½ to 1 pineapple (see note)
1 cup granulated sugar
1 egg, beaten
1½ cups cake flour or 1¼ cups all-purpose flour
2 teaspoons baking powder
⅛ teaspoon salt
¾ cup pineapple juice

Preheat oven to 350°F. In a small bowl, beat brown sugar and 2 tablespoons butter until mixture is well-blended and creamy.

Spray a 9-inch cake pan with vegetable spray and press the sugar mixture against the sides and bottom of the cake pan. Cover bottom of the pan with pineapple rings or pieces and press into the sugar mixture. Make sure that the pineapple pieces cover the bottom of the pan completely.

Combine the remaining butter and granulated sugar and beat until creamy; add the egg and blend well.

In a medium bowl, sift together the cake flour, baking powder, and salt and fold into mixture. Add pineapple juice until mixture has the consistency to make batter.

Pour batter into the fruit-lined cake pan; bake for about 40 to 45 minutes then turn cake out of pan immediately to cool.

Note: This can be made with fresh or canned pineapple.

PINEAPPLE CAKE

Serves 12 to 16

1½ cups granulated sugar
2¼ cups cake flour
1 tablespoon baking powder
2 large eggs
½ cup milk
1½ teaspoons pure vanilla extract
½ cup crushed pineapple
Pineapple Icing

Preheat oven to 350°F. Grease and flour one 9-inch springform pan.

In a large bowl, sift together sugar, flour, and baking powder; set aside. In a small bowl, beat together eggs, milk, and vanilla extract. Add to the flour mixture and mix well to combine. Fold in crushed pineapple and pour into the prepared springform pan. Bake for 40 minutes or until just done. Let cool. Spread icing with a metal spatula.

PINEAPPLE ICING

Makes about ½ cup icing

¼ cup crushed pineapple in heavy syrup
2 ounces cream cheese
1 tablespoon butter
½ teaspoon pure vanilla extract
¾ cup powdered sugar

Bring all ingredients to room temperature. Drain pineapple and reserve syrup.

In a small mixing bowl, combine cream cheese, butter, vanilla extract, and powdered sugar and mix until smooth. Add heavy pineapple syrup until icing reaches the correct consistency. Frost the top of the cooled cake and sprinkle with drained crushed pineapple.

BAKED PINEAPPLE CHEESECAKE

Serves 12 to 16

1½ cups graham cracker crumbs
¼ cup granulated sugar
⅓ cup butter

PINEAPPLE SAUCE
1 (20-ounce) can crushed pineapple in heavy syrup
¼ cup granulated sugar
1½ tablespoons cornstarch
2 tablespoons lemon juice

2 (8-ounce) packages cream cheese
1 (14-ounce) can sweetened condensed milk
3 large eggs
¼ cup fresh lemon juice
Pineapple Sauce

Preheat oven to 300°F. Bring all ingredients to room temperature.

In a medium bowl, combine graham cracker crumbs, sugar, and butter until ingredients are thoroughly mixed. Press crumbs firmly on the bottom of a 9-inch springform pan. Set aside.

To make the Pineapple Sauce, place a strainer over a small bowl and drain crushed pineapple.

In a saucepan, combine syrup, sugar, cornstarch, and lemon juice and simmer for 5 minutes, stirring constantly. Add in crushed pineapple and stir until evenly distributed. Set aside to cool.

Using a hand mixer, beat cream cheese until fluffy. Slowly beat in sweetened condensed milk until smooth. Mix in eggs, lemon juice, and Pineapple Sauce until completely combined. Pour cream cheese filling into the prepared pan. Bake until the center sets (about 55 minutes). Chill overnight.

The Pineapple Sauce by itself is also great served hot over ice cream or bread pudding.

PINEAPPLE CHEESECAKE WITH PINEAPPLE MANGO SAUCE

Serves 12 to 16

1¼ cups graham cracker crumbs
¼ cup granulated sugar
1 teaspoon cinnamon
¼ cup butter
4 (8-ounce) packages cream cheese, softened
1 cup granulated sugar
2 teaspoons lemon juice
1 teaspoon pure vanilla extract
4 large eggs
Pineapple Mango Sauce

Preheat oven to 300°F. Spray a 9-inch springform pan with non-stick vegetable oil cooking spray.

In a medium bowl, combine graham cracker crumbs, sugar, cinnamon, and butter; blend well with fingertips. Press crumbs on the bottom of the prepared springform pan.

In a large mixing bowl, beat cream cheese on low speed until smooth (about 30 seconds). Scrape the bowl after each addition. Add sugar and beat until just blended. Add lemon juice, vanilla extract, and 1 egg and beat together until just blended. Continue to add remaining eggs, 1 egg at a time, and beat until just blended.

Pour cheesecake filling over crust and smooth with a spatula. Bake 60 to 75 minutes (sides will be firm but center may still be slightly soft). Place the cake pan on a wire rack and cool completely. Cover and chill in the refrigerator overnight.

Once plated, pour Pineapple Mango Sauce on top. Serve.

PINEAPPLE MANGO SAUCE

Makes about 1 cup

½ cup crushed pineapple in heavy syrup
½ cup mango flesh
2 teaspoons granulated sugar

Drain and reserve syrup from pineapple. Purée pineapple and mango in the food processor. Heat fruit mixture with sugar over low temperature until sauce thickens. Cool before serving.

PINEAPPLE CHERRY CREAM CHEESE PIE

Serves 8

- 1 (8-ounce) package cream cheese, softened
- 1 (14-ounce) can sweetened condensed milk
- ⅓ cup lemon juice from concentrate
- 1 teaspoon almond extract
- 1 (8-inch) graham cracker crust (see note)
- 2 cups crushed pineapple in heavy syrup
- 1 cup canned sweetened cherry pie filling

In a large bowl, whisk together softened cream cheese and sweetened condensed milk. Once blended, stir in lemon juice and almond extract. Pour into graham cracker crust and chill overnight or until set (about 4 hours).

Place a kitchen strainer over a small bowl and drain crushed pineapple. Reserve syrup for other use.

Just before serving, carefully spoon the cherry pie filling around the outer edge of the pie. Then spoon the drained crushed pineapple into the center and spread evenly. Serve.

Note: Store-bought premade pie crusts make this dessert a cinch.

SLOW-BAKING CHEWY PINEAPPLE COOKIES

Makes 3 dozen

2 cups all-purpose flour
1 teaspoon baking soda
1 teaspoon salt
1 cup dry rolled oats
½ cup unsalted butter
½ cup unsweetened applesauce
2 large eggs
1 teaspoon pure vanilla extract
¾ cup granulated sugar
¾ cup dark brown sugar
1 cup chocolate chips
1 cup well-drained pineapple, crushed
½ cup crushed walnuts
¾ cup loose raisins

Preheat oven to 300°F and allow ingredients to reach room temperature.

In a medium mixing bowl, combine flour, baking soda, salt, and oats and set aside.

In a separate medium mixing bowl, combine butter, applesauce, eggs, and vanilla extract and beat until creamy. Add the granulated sugar and brown sugar and beat until smooth. Gradually add flour mixture into butter-sugar mixture until thoroughly mixed. Stir in chocolate chips, pineapple, walnuts, and raisins.

Drop rounded teaspoons of cookie dough onto an ungreased cookie sheet. Place the cookie sheet in the oven and bake for 18 to 20 minutes, or until golden brown. Remove from the oven and let the sheet stand for 2 minutes and then move cookies to wire racks to cool.

PINEAPPLE MERINGUE SURPRISE KISSES

Makes 2 dozen

3 large egg whites
⅛ teaspoon salt
⅛ teaspoon cream of tartar
¾ cup granulated sugar
½ teaspoon pure vanilla extract
¼ cup mini semisweet chocolate chips
2 tablespoons fresh or canned crushed pineapple, drained well

Preheat oven to 300°F. Cover cookie sheet with parchment paper.

Whisk or beat egg whites until foamy. Beat in salt and cream of tartar and gradually beat in sugar (about 2 tablespoons at a time) until stiff. Fold in vanilla extract. Using teaspoons, drop kisses onto the prepared cookie sheet. Make a small valley in the center of each cookie; place a few chocolate chips and about ¼ teaspoon pineapple. Bake for 30 minutes and turn off oven; leave cookies in the oven for 45 to 60 minutes to dry.

PINEAPPLE TAPIOCA PUDDING WITH TOASTED COCONUT

Serves 2

1 (13-ounce) can coconut milk
1 cup canned crushed pineapple with juice
1 cup granulated sugar
¼ cup quick-cooking tapioca
1 large egg, beaten
½ cup sweetened flaked coconut (see note)

In a heavy-bottomed saucepan, combine coconut milk, pineapple, sugar, tapioca, and beaten egg. Mix well and let sit for 5 minutes.

Cook tapioca over medium heat, stirring constantly. Once it reaches a full boil, remove from heat. Cool for 20 minutes. Top with toasted coconut and serve warm, or cover and refrigerate and serve cold.

Note: To toast coconut, place flaked coconut in a small ungreased nonstick pan. Then cook over medium heat and stir constantly until lightly browned. Cool on paper towels.

PINEAPPLE SORBET

Serves 2

2 cups water
2 cups granulated sugar
2 cups crushed pineapple in juice (see note)
½ cup fresh lemon juice

Boil water and sugar together for 5 minutes. Add crushed pineapple and lemon juice and allow to cool. Strain through a piece of damp cheesecloth. Reserve pineapple in the refrigerator for garnish.

Pour into a 10 x 13-inch pan and stir ice crystals at least once an hour to create smaller, smoother ice crystals.

Scoop sorbet and top with reserved pineapple.

Note: Pineapple juice can be used in place of pineapple in juice.

RUM GRILLED PINEAPPLE Á LA MODE

Serves 4

4 (½-inch) slices fresh pineapple
½ cup rum
2 tablespoons lime juice
2 tablespoons dark brown sugar
1 cup vanilla ice cream

GARNISH

1 teaspoon dark brown sugar

Prepare grill or hibachi for grilling (see note). Slice pineapple and set aside.

In a bowl, combine rum, lime juice, and brown sugar. Marinate pineapple slices for about 30 minutes. Toss occasionally to ensure even coverage.

Over an open flame, grill pineapple until the fruit is tender (about 5 minutes). With a spatula, carefully transfer pineapple onto a plate and remove core.

Place each hot pineapple ring into a wide-mouthed bowl and top with a dollop of vanilla ice cream. Sprinkle with a hint of brown sugar for drama and serve immediately.

Note: In an oven, place pineapple on a nonstick pan and broil for 3 minutes. Turn over and broil for another 3 minutes, or until lightly browned.

CANDIED PINEAPPLE AND GINGER

Makes about 2 cups

4 thumbs fresh ginger root (about 1 cup sliced)
Water for boiling ginger and pineapple
1 cup fresh pineapple, sliced
1 cup granulated sugar
½ cup water for syrup
¼ cup superfine granulated sugar (see note)

Peel and slice ginger across the grain into thin slices. In a saucepan, cover with cold water for 5 minutes and drain. Cover again with cold water and boil for 5 minutes; drain. Spread ginger slices on clean paper towels.

In a saucepan, place pineapple slices in water and boil for 10 to 15 minutes, or until soft. Cut into bite-size candy pieces.

In a medium saucepan, combine 1 cup sugar and water and stir until sugar dissolves. Bring syrup to a boil and carefully add ginger and sliced pineapple. Lower heat and cook gently for 20 minutes, or until most of the syrup has been absorbed. Drain over a coarse sieve.

Roll ginger and pineapple (a few pieces at a time) in fine granulated sugar. Allow to dry and then store in an airtight container.

Note: To make superfine sugar, place 1 cup of granulated sugar in a blender and run the blender for about 1 minute.

PHOTO CREDITS

Adobe Firefly: pages 11, 23, 28, 33, 37, 62, 79, 81, 85, 99, 101, 103

Dreamstime.com: cover, pages 6, 83

Ray Wong: pages 12, 17, 18, 24, 31, 41, 46, 49, 53, 55, 58, 66, 69, 71, 91, 95, 97